INVENTING THE
CELL PHONE

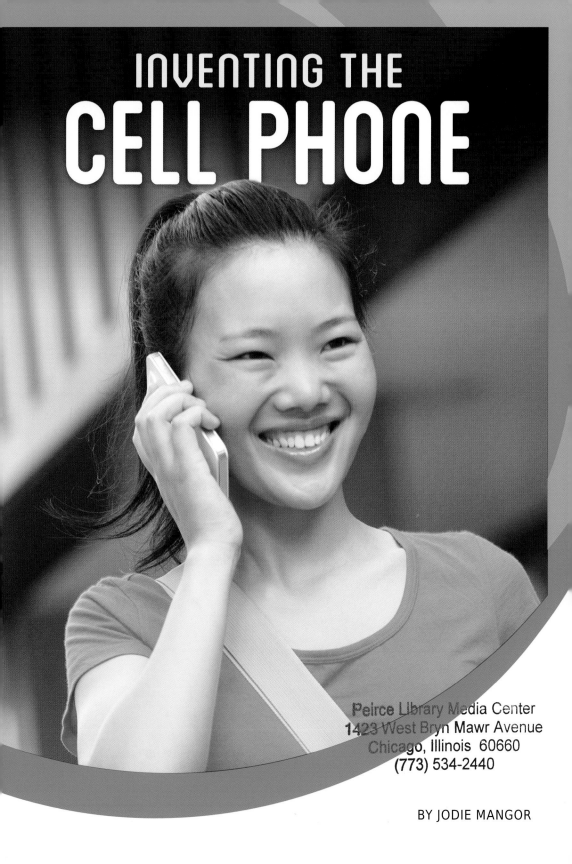

BY JODIE MANGOR

Published by The Child's World®
1980 Lookout Drive • Mankato, MN 56003-1705
800-599-READ • www.childsworld.com

Acknowledgments
The Child's World®: Mary Berendes, Publishing Director
Red Line Editorial: Design, editorial direction, and production
Photographs ©: iStockphoto/Thinkstock, cover, 1; Eric Risberg/AP Images, 4;
Sandy Huffaker/Corbis, 7; Hulton-Deutsch Collection/Corbis, 8; AP Images, 11;
Shutterstock Images, 12, 15 (center); Bryan Solomon/Shutterstock Images, 15 (top), 15
(bottom), 15 (right); Stockbyte/Thinkstock, 16; Jerome Brunet/ZumaPress/Corbis, 18;
iStockphoto, 21

ISBN 9781634074551

LCCN 2015946288

Printed in the United States of America
Mankato, MN
December, 2015
PA02284

ABOUT THE AUTHOR

Jodie Mangor's stories, poems, and articles have appeared in a variety of
children's magazines, and she has authored audio tour scripts for high-profile
museums and tourist destinations around the world. Many of these tours are
for kids. She also puts her degrees in microbiology, environmental science,
and molecular biology to work by editing papers for publication in scientific
journals. She lives in Ithaca, New York, with her family.

TABLE OF
CONTENTS

Chapter 1

A HISTORIC CALL

Marty Cooper was about to do something no one had ever done. The year was 1973. Cooper stood on a sidewalk in New York City and took out his phone. It was the size of a brick. It weighed more than 2 pounds (1 kg). It was the first handheld cell phone ever made. Cooper had helped invent it at a small company called Motorola.

Cooper dialed on the phone. He called his rival, Joel Engel. Engel was also racing to invent a cell phone. He worked for Bell Labs. Bell Labs was part of the giant phone company AT&T. Cooper wanted to let Engel know that Motorola was ahead in the race.

Cooper said, "Joel, this is Marty. I'm calling you from a cell phone. A real, handheld, portable cell phone."[1]

Engel was quiet. He was unhappy that his rival had beaten him. But the race was not over!

◀ **Marty Cooper holds the first cell phone that he and his team created.**

Cooper's phone was a major step in the history of cell phones. But it was only a sample phone. It was big and heavy. It had to be charged for ten hours to talk on it for 35 minutes. And it was very expensive. The phone was not ready to be sold to the public. Ten more years would pass before Motorola or AT&T sold handheld cell phones.

The race was not just between Cooper and Engel. Others wanted to make cell phones, too. And they were making progress!

Cooper sits with samples of early cell phones. ▶

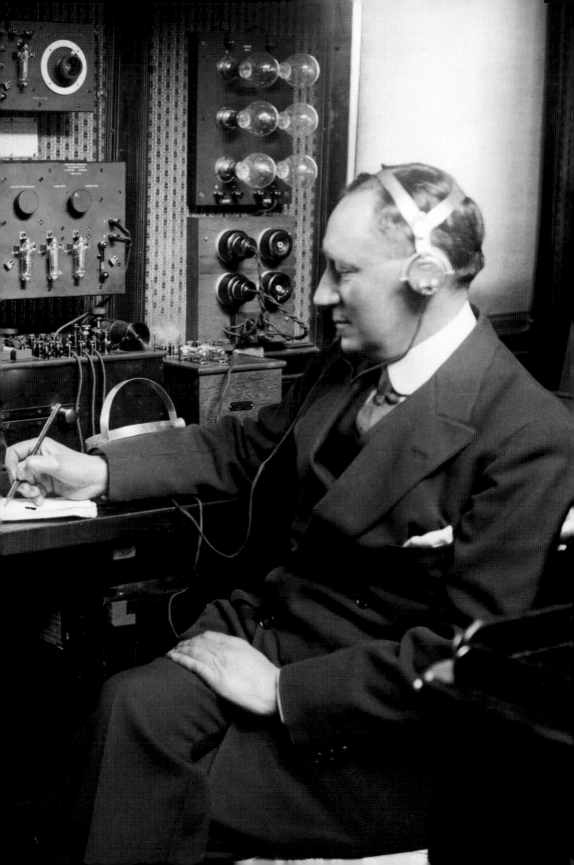

Chapter 2

RACING WITH RADIO WAVES

Marty Cooper is known for inventing the first cell phone. But he did not do it alone. Many people helped. They built on previous technologies. And there were lots of steps along the way.

In the late 1800s in Italy, Guglielmo Marconi made an exciting discovery. He found that radio waves could carry sounds. He built special radios. They could send and receive messages in Morse code.

Marconi's radios were wireless. Before his invention, wires had been used to carry sounds from one place to another. Landline telephones needed a network of wires to work. But Marconi's radios did not. Today's cell phones are also wireless. Like Marconi's radios, they use radio waves to carry sound.

Marconi put his radios in ships. People did not believe the radios could send long-distance messages. But they could. In

◄ Guglielmo Marconi won the Nobel Prize for inventing the wireless radio.

1901, Marconi sent radio signals all the way across the Atlantic Ocean. He said he was sure that one day people "would be able to send messages without wires . . . between the farthermost ends of the earth."[2]

These radios were a great invention. They helped keep ships safe. They were also a first step toward making a cell phone.

By the 1930s, some American police had **two-way** radios in their cars. These radios let people in different cars talk to each other. This made it easier to communicate. But the radios were not true phones. They could not connect to the wired telephone system.

After World War II (1939–1945), inventors got even closer to making a portable cell phone. They made wireless radio car phones. These car phones could connect to the wired telephone system. Now people on house phones and car phones could call each other. But the car phones were very big. They filled a car's trunk. They needed a lot of power to work. And they cost more than a new car!

The race to make a handheld wireless phone was on. Some inventors worked to make the phones smaller. Some worked to create a battery with longer life. And others worked on the problem of many users and not enough radio waves to carry their calls.

▲ A New York police officer holds a two-way radio
in the 1930s.

One of these people was D. H. Ring. He came up with a key

idea. Without it, today's cell phones could not exist.

Chapter 3

FROM CELL TO CELL

In 1947, engineer D. H. Ring had a great idea. It would solve two big problems. And it would turn wireless phones into cell phones.

A wireless phone is a kind of two-way radio. To work, it needs radio waves. The U.S. government controls the country's radio waves. It lets phone companies use only a small part of all the radio waves. So, this was the first problem. How could many calls be carried by so few waves?

A wireless phone also needs a base station to work. A base station sends and receives phone signals. A phone will stop working if it is too far away from the station. So, this was the second problem. How could wireless phones be made to work in more places?

Ring's idea was to divide an area of land into smaller shapes. Each shape is a few square miles in size. It is called a cell. Each

◀ Some base stations are in fields, while others are in cities.

cell has its own base station. All base stations are linked to a control office. This office connects cell phone calls to the main telephone system.

As a person moves from cell to cell, calls are passed from base station to base station. With cells, radio waves can be used more than once. And with many small base stations, people can use their phones in more places. These cells gave the cell phone its name.

Even using Ring's idea, there was still work to be done. But the finish line was getting closer. Soon people would be able to buy and use cell phones.

BASE STATIONS AND CELLS

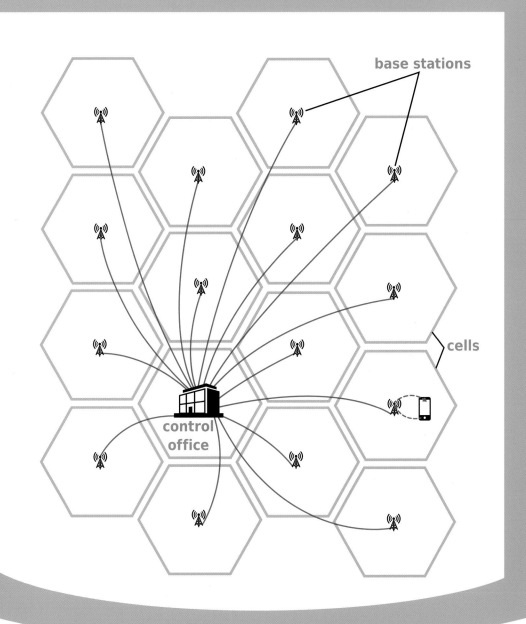

base stations

cells

control
office

Chapter 4

CELL PHONES TAKE OFF

Marty Cooper and Joel Engel worked hard to make cell phones. So did other Americans. Thanks to them, the United States was ahead in the race. Soon it would have a public cell phone system.

The finish line was very close. But first the U.S. government had to approve cell phone systems. It gave out licenses that allowed companies to set up cell phone systems. At one point, there were 92,000 companies applying for the final 180 licenses. The government took years to hand out the licenses. This gave other countries a chance to catch up.

In 1981, the race came to an end. Sweden and its neighbors Norway, Denmark, and Finland introduced the first public cell phone system. Two years later, the United States had its own cell phone system. Each phone cost almost $10,000 in today's money. But some people bought them anyway. Over time, more cell phone systems were built. By the 1990s, the price of phones dropped. Cell phone systems spread far and wide.

◄ By the mid-1990s, cell phones were small enough to fit in a pocket.

By the 2000s, even people in the poorest areas of the world had cell phones. Wired phone systems cost a lot. But people could afford cell phones. They found that cell phones could even work in places with no electricity. People could charge their phones with car batteries. Workers set up base stations that ran on diesel fuel or solar power. People went from having no phones to having cell phones.

Engineers kept designing new cell phones. Each one was better than the last. Cell phones became smaller. They worked better. And they cost less.

In 2007, Steve Jobs of Apple stepped onto a stage. The event was Apple's annual conference. Jobs stood in front of a crowd and pulled out a new product. It would change the world of cell phones. It was the first iPhone. Jobs said, "After today I don't think anyone is going to look at these phones in the same way."[3]

The iPhone is a kind of smartphone. Smartphones have computer chips that turn them into mini computers. Smartphones can be used to do many things. Users can get on the Internet and stream videos. They can send text messages. They can also take photos, play games, and listen to music.

◄ Steve Jobs introduces the iPhone in 2007.

The iPhone was not the first smartphone. But the iPhone was very easy to use. Users could do many things by touching the screen. The iPhone helped make smartphones popular. Jobs said, "I want to make a phone that people will love."[4] And he did.

Today, people all over the world use cell phones. The world has seven billion people. There are more than six billion cell phones. In many countries, there are more cell phones than people. Millions of base stations help the cell phones work. They are not always nice to look at. Sometimes they are disguised to blend in. Some have been made to look like trees, flagpoles, or even cacti.

Today's cell phones are made by companies from all over the world. Both Samsung and LG are from South Korea. Apple is American. Xiaomi and Lenovo are from China. Sony Ericsson is from Japan and Sweden. Nokia is from Finland. Cell phone parts are also made all over the world. One phone could have parts from Australia, Africa, South America, North America, Asia, and Europe!

Cell phones help families and friends keep in touch. They make it easier to do business. They are good to have in an emergency. And they can provide entertainment. Cell phones are powerful tools. They have changed our lives.

What will the future look like? What will new cell phones be able to do? One thing is certain. A future with more cell phones is calling to us.

▲ A base station is disguised as a palm tree.

GLOSSARY

base station (BAYS STAY-shun): A base station is a place with equipment that connects cell phones to the regular phone system. A cell phone tower is sometimes part of a base station.

computer chips (kum-PYOO-tur CHIPS): Computer chips are very small electronic circuits that can send information. Smartphones have computer chips inside them.

Morse code (MORS KOHD): Morse code is a system of long and short sounds that stand for letters and numbers. Before wireless radios were invented, people used Morse code to send messages.

radio waves (RAY-dee-oh WAYVZ): Radio waves are a kind of signal that travels through the air without using wires. Cell phones need radio waves to work.

solar power (SOH-lur POW-ur): Solar power is energy that comes from the sun. Scientists built phone systems that can use solar power.

two-way (TOO-whey): Two-way means able to send and receive messages. People can use two-way radios to talk to each other from far away.

wireless (WY-ur-less): Wireless means not using wires to send and receive electronic signals. Cell phones are wireless.

TO LEARN MORE

Books

Berger, Melvin, and Gilda Berger. *Did You Invent the Phone Alone, Alexander Graham Bell?* New York: Scholastic, 2007.

Hantula, Richard. *How Do Cell Phones Work?* New York: Chelsea Clubhouse, 2009.

Higgins, Nadia. *How Cell Phones Work.* Mankato, MN: The Child's World, 2012.

Kling, Andrew A. *Cell Phones.* Farmington Hills, MI: Lucent Books, 2010.

Web Sites

Visit our Web site for links about cell phones: childsworld.com/links

Note to Parents, Teachers, and Librarians: We routinely verify our Web links to make sure they are safe and active sites. So encourage your readers to check them out!

SOURCE NOTES

1. Tom Geoghegan. "Twitter, Telegram and E-mail: Famous First Lines." *BBC*. BBC, 21 Mar. 2011. Web. 24 Jul. 2015.

2. "Marconi receives radio signal over Atlantic." *PBS*. PBS, n.d. Web. 24 Jul. 2015.

3. John Markoff. "Apple Introduces Innovative Cellphone." *New York Times*. New York Times Company, 10 Jan. 2007. Web. 24 Jul. 2015.

4. John Lasseter. "Fond Farewells: Steve Jobs." *Time*. Time, Inc., 14 Dec. 2011. Web. 24 Jul. 2015.

INDEX